39

Pennycook El
3620 Fernwood Street
Vallejo, CA 94591
707-556-8590

W9-CTN-804

Consumers and Producers

Ellen K. Mitten

rourkeeducationalmedia.com

© 2012 Rourke Educational Media

All rights reserved. No part of this book may be reproduced or utilized in any form or by any means, electronic or mechanical including photocopying, recording, or by any information storage and retrieval system without permission in writing from the publisher.

www.rourkeeducationalmedia.com

PHOTO CREDITS: Cover: © Nicu Mircea, Zelijko Santrac; Title Page, 3, 21: © Andres Rodriguez; Page 4: © Michael Gray, Natalia Nazarenko Vladimirovna; Page 5: © Natalia Nazarekno Vladimirovna, James Phelps Jr., Michael Flippo; Page 6: © Galina Barskaya; Page 7: © Godfer; Page 8: © laflor; Page 9: © DOUGBERRY; Page 10: © Alistair Cotton, Sean Locke; Page 11: © kali9, webphotographeer; Page 12: © Alena Ozerova; Page 13: © Hippylee; Page 14: © PeterPhoto, malerapaso; Page 15: © Barcin; Page 17: © Kristina Afanasyeva; Page 19: © Wavebreakmedia Ltd; Page 22: © RBFried, egalegal; Page 23: © Maros Markovic;

Edited by: Meg Greve

Cover design by Tara Ramo
Interior design by Teri Intzegian

Library of Congress Cataloging-in-Publication Data

Mitten, Ellen K.
 Consumers and Producers / Ellen K. Mitten
    p. cm. -- (Little World Social Studies)
 Includes bibliographical references and index.
 ISBN 978-1-61741-790-0 (hard cover) (alk. paper)
 ISBN 978-1-61741-992-8 (soft cover)
 Library of Congress Control Number: 2011924835

Rourke Educational Media
Printed in the United States of America,
North Mankato, Minnesota

Educational Media

rourkeeducationalmedia.com

customerservice@rourkeeducationalmedia.com • PO Box 643328 Vero Beach, Florida 32964

Do you or your family buy games or pay for haircuts? If you buy or pay for anything, then you are a **consumer**.

We call all the things we buy **goods** and **services**. Goods are things that you can touch and use.

Services are something someone does for you.

All the people who make the goods or provide the services are called **producers**.

Everyone can be both a consumer and a producer.

PRODUCER
of Vegetables

CONSUMER
of Vegetables

CONSUMER
of a Service

PRODUCER
of a Service

You might be a producer, too.

Do you sell lemonade or walk your neighbor's dog?

Producers get paid for the goods or services they provide.

When selling goods or services, producers want to make money, or a profit.

When buying goods or services, consumers want to pay a fair amount.

SALE UP TO 80%

The buying and selling that consumers and producers do makes a **system**. We call the system the **economy**.

Have you been a consumer or producer in the economy today?

Picture Glossary

consumer (kuhn-SOO-mur): Someone who buys and uses products and services.

economy (i-KON-uh-mee): The way a country runs its system of goods and services.

goods (gudz): Things that are sold, or things that someone owns, as in leather goods or household goods.

 **producers** (pruh-DOOSS-urz): People who make or manufacture goods, or provide a service.

 **services** (SUR-viss-iz): Work that helps others.

 **system** (SIS-tuhm): Things that work together in a connected, organized way.

Index

Websites

www.socialstudiesforkids.com

www.youngmoney.com

www.ftc.gov/youarehere

About the Author

Ellen K. Mitten has been teaching four and five year-olds since 1995. She and her family love reading all sorts of books!